THE RESTORATION STATION

A three- to five-day holiday club based on John's Gospel

From Scripture Union

For 5- to 11-year-olds

© Scripture Union 2022

First published 2022

ISBN 978 1 78506 915 4

Scripture Union
Trinity House, Opal Court, Opal Drive,
Fox Milne, Milton Keynes MK15 0DF
Email: info@scriptureunion.org.uk
Website: www.scriptureunion.org.uk

All rights reserved. No part of this publication may be reproduced, stored in a retrieval system, or transmitted in any form or by any means, electronic, mechanical, photocopying, recording or otherwise, without the prior permission of Scripture Union.

The right of Sue Clutterham to be identified as author of this work has been asserted by her in accordance with the Copyright, Designs and Patents Act 1988.

Scripture quotations from the Holy Bible, New Living Translation, copyright © 1996. Used by permission of Tyndale House Publishers, Inc., Wheaton, Illinois 60189 USA. All rights reserved.

British Library Cataloguing-in-Publication Data

A catalogue record of this book is available from the British Library.

Printed in India by Nutech Print Services

Cover and internal design: kwgraphicdesign

Writer: Sue Clutterham

Scripture Union is an international Christian charity working with churches in more than 130 countries. Thank you for purchasing this book. Any profits from this book support SU in England and Wales to bring the good news of Jesus Christ to children, young people and families and to enable them to meet God through the Bible and prayer.

Find out more about our work and how you can get involved at:

- www.scriptureunion.org.uk (England and Wales)
- www.suscotland.org.uk (Scotland)
- www.suni.co.uk (Northern Ireland)
- www.scriptureunion.org (USA)
- www.su.org.au (Australia)

For two little boys who have brought so much joy into our lives as they have begun their journey with Jesus, the great restorer.

CONTENTS

The Basics

Welcome — 6
Who is this for? — 7
A different approach — 8
An ongoing strategy — 9

Overview and Bible programme — 10
Who is Jesus the Restorer? — 10
Bible Workshops — 11

Programme — 12
Programme elements — 12
Programme timetable — 14
Restoration Toolkit — 15

The team — 16
Team roles — 16

The children — 18
Getting to know the children — 18
Asking questions — 19
Children with additional needs — 19
Children from other faiths — 19
Children from a 5% background — 20
Workbench teams — 20
Talking with children about healing and brokenness — 22

Setting up — 24
Registration and collection — 24
Upfront area — 25
Workbench team areas — 25
Explore deeper areas — 25

Resources — 26
Additional workshops — 26
Booklets for children — 26
Drama scripts — 27
Daisy and Dan animations — 27
Publicity — 27
Other downloadable resources — 27
Legal requirements and safeguarding — 27

Follow up — 28
What next? — 28
Faith journeys — 29

The Workshops

Workshop 1 — 32
Jesus meets a very important man
Schedule — 33
Drama 1 — 38
Board game – photocopiable page — 40
Bible verse jigsaw – photocopiable page — 41

Workshop 2 — 42
Jesus meets a man who can't walk
Schedule — 43
Drama 2 — 48
Jointed figure – photocopiable page — 50
Lame man – photocopiable page — 51

Workshop 3 — 52
Jesus restores Peter
Schedule — 53
Drama 3 — 58

Workbench shouts
Photocopiable pages — 60

THE BASICS

WELCOME
TO **THE RESTORATION STATION**

Imagine you have a treasured possession – a family heirloom. Over the years it has become faded – possibly torn or broken, or even completely spoiled. One day, you discover that a renowned restorer is in town and is willing to repair anything and everything. Of course, you take your valuable item to them, trusting that they will make it like new once more.

Jesus wants to meet us where we are, forgive us for the stuff that needs sorting out and restore us to wholeness and new life in him! Jesus said, 'I came so they can have real and eternal life, more and better life than they ever dreamed of' (John 10:10, *The Message*).

Welcome to **The Restoration Station**! Help the children meet with Jesus as they become crafters at workbenches. Each day they will explore a story about Jesus healing and restoring some very different people, including the son of an important official, a blind man and his friend, Peter.

Who is this for?

The focus of Scripture Union's work is on the 95% of children and young people who are not in church (we'll refer to them as 'children from the 95' or 'the 95' from here on). So, we have written this holiday club material with these children, who perhaps know very little about Jesus, as the target group.

We want to help you and your team connect with the 95 and give them an opportunity to explore who Jesus is and respond to him in appropriate ways. Of course, our prayer is that, ultimately, they will become lifelong followers of Jesus, although we don't expect this will necessarily happen during one holiday club! We recommend that a holiday club is part of an integrated, ongoing strategy for mission and engagement with the 95. We'll think more about this a little later.

We also hope that this holiday club will help and encourage churched children, and young people working as helpers, to explore and respond further, and to grow in faith, too. Information on adapting the content for

WELCOME

WELCOME

REVEALING JESUS

The **Revealing Jesus** mission framework is designed to help you journey into faith with the 95% of children and young people not in church.

We've identified four stages on the journey that most people follow as they engage with Christianity: **Connect**, **Explore**, **Respond** and **Grow**.

The framework provides shaping principles for each stage, but also offers flexibility in expression as we recognise that contexts, and children and young people themselves, vary hugely.

Find out more at: **https://content.scriptureunion.org.uk/revealingjesus.**

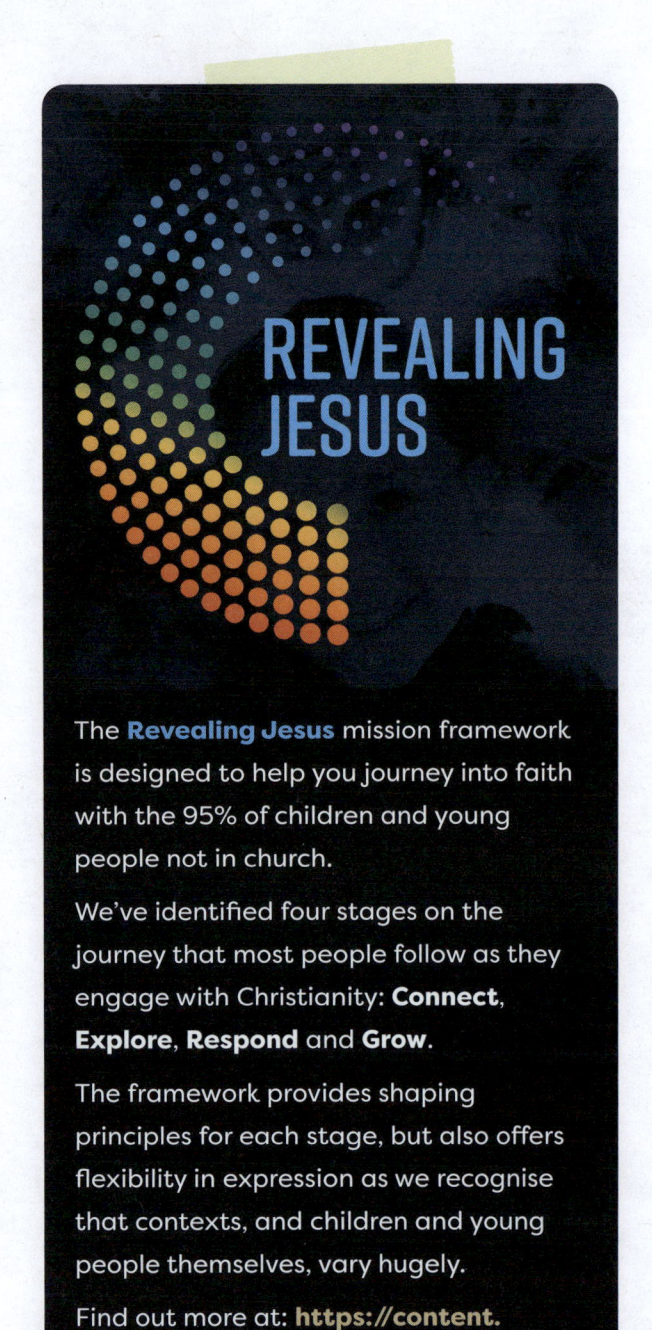

children who are already connected to church can be found on page 20.

Before you go any further, the most important thing to do is pray! If possible during the build-up to The Restoration Station, pray regularly for each child and team member by name.

A different approach

We recognise that times have changed and, increasingly, families have extremely busy lives. As a result, many churches are now running events differently. We have provided material for three sessions in this book, with material for a further two sessions available online. The outline here is complete, and the additional days are just that: they add to what is already in the book, but the programme works without them. Each session stands on its own, which means, for example, that the five sessions *could* be spread throughout the year, but equally they could be completed during a single week. The choice is yours!

Other changes we have made to this material are to make it more appropriate for children from the 95.

Imagine yourself going to an event that you've never been to before. You don't know many, if any, people there and the building is unfamiliar; you're not quite sure what happens, yet everyone else seems to know what to do, so it feels a bit threatening. This may well be the experience of children from the 95 coming to The Restoration Station, so bear this in mind as you plan and prepare. Make sure the team are aware that some children may feel daunted as they arrive at The Restoration Station, and discuss appropriate ways that they could help the children to feel at ease. Some of the things we have done to help include:

CHURCH SERVICES

There are no outlines for a Sunday service. Although it's important to link children into a church if practical and possible, that often takes time. A standard church service at the end of a holiday club week will be very unfamiliar to the 95, not least because it will be very different from **The Restoration Station**. This material does not have an outline for a church service, as such. However, you might want to organise a family activity to which children who attended **The Restoration Station** and church families are all invited, giving them the chance to build relationships with each other (and it could be in the church building!).

STORIES

The material focuses on stories from John's Gospel that might be very familiar to churched children, but not to the 95. As we have turned things on their head, you may find it helpful to read the section on working with the 5% on page 20.

DAISY AND DAN

Stories of healing and restoration can raise some big questions for children as they look at brokenness in the world around them and, possibly, in their own family situations. Each day an animation featuring the characters Daisy and Dan will help to explore how Jesus can be present in brokenness. The article 'Talking with children about healing and brokenness' on pages 22 and 23 offers extra guidance on this potentially difficult topic.

SINGING

We haven't suggested that you have a band, as it wouldn't necessarily be appropriate to ask children who know little about Jesus to sing songs of worship. However, children do love singing, so if you know good songs that are suitable and complement the Bible exploration, and don't require the children to sing things they may not yet believe, you could sing those. If possible, use accompanying videos and also actions, so the children are engaged in the music.

LEARNING STYLES

Children learn in different ways, so we've provided material for them to explore the story in three different ways: talking, creating and thinking. Each day there will be questions to ponder that will help the children in their exploration. This exploring is self-led, and the leaders are there to help, not to impose activities.

An ongoing strategy

We're so pleased you've chosen to share the good news of Jesus with the children and young people in your community! **The Restoration Station** is designed to be part of an ongoing strategy. It's great to organise a successful and exciting event, but what will happen next for the children you reach out to? Make sure you begin your planning by answering these questions:

- How committed can you be to maintaining contact long term with the children who attend?
- Can you arrange follow-up activities for the children that will include their families?

OVERVIEW
AND **BIBLE PROGRAMME**

Who is Jesus the Restorer?

This holiday club invites children to explore who Jesus the Restorer is. Each day unpacks a new miracle, healing or restoration told through the stories found in John's Gospel, helping the children to see who Jesus is, the difference he makes in the lives of the people he meets and what that might mean for the children themselves.

Bible Workshops

WORKSHOP 1
Jesus meets a very important man
John 4:46–53

In this first session the children will start to explore who this man called Jesus is, and how he was a restorer and seemingly able to do things that were impossible. Through the activities and discussions in the session they will learn how Jesus was able to heal people without even being with them. They will also explore the theme of God as a rock and a firm foundation who we can rely on when things feel uncertain.

WORKSHOP 2
Jesus meets a man who can't walk
John 5:1–13

The children will hear about Jesus meeting and healing a man who couldn't walk, and begin to understand that Jesus can fix and restore people who are seemingly broken. They will be encouraged to think about being broken on the inside as well as in their physical bodies.

WORKSHOP 3
Jesus restores Peter
John 21:3–17

The children learn how Peter, even though he was one of Jesus' closest friends, let Jesus down and denied that he even knew him. The activities and discussions in the session explore the concepts of forgiveness and being made whole again. The children will hear how Jesus restores Peter, and be encouraged to think about how he might restore them.

Additional Workshops
(online only)

If you wish to run your holiday club for four or five days, extra content enabling you to do this can be found online at **su.org.uk/TheRestorationStation**.

The additional Workshop(s) can be added into the programme between Workshops 2 and 3 – thus expanding the amount of time children spend exploring how Jesus heals and restores by looking at his encounters with others. You can do either or both of the additional Workshops: they stand alone but add to the overall understanding of who Jesus is.

ADDITIONAL WORKSHOP A
Jesus brings Lazarus back to life
John 11:1–44

In the first of the two extra sessions, the children build on the idea that Jesus can bring new life when they hear the story of Jesus bringing Lazarus back to life. The activities and discussions in the session also explore how God can be our shelter and our refuge when things in life seem really tough.

ADDITIONAL WORKSHOP B
Jesus heals a blind man
John 9:1–11

Sometimes things in our lives may be sad or dark – for lots of reasons. Through hearing about Jesus' healing of a blind man the children will be encouraged to understand that Jesus wants to help them, just like he helped the blind man. He wants to take away the darkness and bring light; anyone who belongs to Jesus will become a new person. The old life is gone; a new life has begun!

PROGRAMME
BREAKDOWN AND TIMINGS

An outline of the suggested programme is given in the table on page 14 and the different elements are described briefly below. The Workshops, starting on page 32, give you activity material for each of these elements, for the three core Workshops of the club. Material for two Additional Workshops is available online at **su.org.uk/The RestorationStation**. The material in each Workshop will last for about two and a quarter hours, in a mixture of all-together, exploring and small-group time, but can be adapted to suit your context and the children you are working with. During the club the children will be divided into Workbench teams of up to ten. More details about Workbench teams can be found on page 20.

Programme elements

TEAM TIME
(30 minutes)

The team is your most valuable resource. Meet well in advance of each session's start time and begin with a focus on the Bible story for that day, before praying for the children, all leaders and helpers, and the activities. After that, sort out any last-minute practicalities before the children arrive!

CLOCK-IN
(10 minutes)

When the children arrive, they should be welcomed and given a name badge, and assigned to a Workbench team. You could date-stamp a card for each child, to give the feel of a real clock-in desk.

WORKBENCH WELCOME
(20 minutes)

The Workbench Leaders and Helpers should welcome each child by name and invite them to join in with the opening activity. It's important to start building a rapport between the Workbench Leaders and the children in their group during this time. Leaders need to look out for children who may not be as confident as others, to make sure they feel included.

LISTEN UP!
(10 minutes)

The children are welcomed from the front by one or two Presenters (adult leaders) who introduce themselves. At this point, any announcements for the day are made, including arrangements for going to the toilet and the location of fire exits.

THE RESTORATION STATION WORKOUT
(5 minutes)

The workout is an opportunity for the children to let off steam before settling down to listen to the Bible story! A team member leads some simple exercises, such as star jumps, running on the spot and so on. Have appropriate, possibly prerecorded, music with a good beat, and a way of playing this so it can be heard (make sure your organisation has the appropriate licence for public playing of recorded music). Make sure the activity is fun and relaxed and, as with all the activities, the team should also join in with the children. If you think you may end up running late, or there is too much in the programme, this activity could be omitted or shortened.

EXPLORE!
(20 minutes)

The children first hear the day's Bible story during 'Explore!', with the introductory activity from 'Workbench Welcome' being referred to in some way. The drama for each day follows on from the story, drawing out the key ideas; the short Daisy and Dan animation (see page 27) will explore one of the big questions that some children may ask after hearing the story.

EXPLORE DEEPER
(5–10 minutes)

At this point in the session the children are offered some questions to help them think more about what they have just seen and heard, and three different ways of exploring the questions. It is important to make this a free choice – the children can choose whichever approach suits them best.

- **Talking** In a group or groups with an Exploring Guide, this is an opportunity to answer any questions the children may have, as well as using the questions provided. Try not to stifle the children's responses, particularly if their ideas are misguided. Gently and sensitively share your own thoughts and responses with the children, helping them to understand a view that differs from their own. Allow thought and imagination to flow and ask more questions when a child answers a question. Help them to explore God's Word for themselves!

- **Creating** Here the children explore the questions, and their own responses, using images and creative materials.

- **Thinking** A space, set up away from the noise and chatter of the other groups, where children choose to think quietly and reflect on everything they have seen and heard.

SNACK BREAK
(10 minutes)

The refreshments could be served to each team at their Workbench team table. It's a good time to chat while enjoying a drink and a snack together.

WORKBENCH EXPLORATION
(50 minutes)

In their Workbench teams, the children do two activities to help them think further about the Workshop themes.

- **Go for it!** A chance to play some games (that relate to the story) and for the children to move around. The suggested games need space and are ideally played outside! However, it is possible to organise them indoors as well.
- **Restoration information** The children explore the story using their *Toolbox* and *Logbook* notebooks.

FINISH UP
(5 minutes)

The presenter concludes the session, summing up what the children have done and possibly saying a prayer. The children are then collected.

TEAM DEBRIEF
(10 minutes)

Once all the children have been collected, the team gathers to debrief, pray for the children and make preparations for the next session.

Programme timetable

TIMING	ACTIVITY	CHILDREN	TEAM
BEFORE CLUB BEGINS			
30 mins	Team time		All team
10 mins	Clock-in	Individually	Registration team
CLUB BEGINS			
Small-group time			
20 mins	Workbench welcome	Small groups	Workbench Leaders and Helpers
Together time			
10 mins	Listen up!	All together	Presenters
5 mins	The Restoration Station workout	All together	Presenters
20 mins	Explore!	All together	Presenters
Exploring time			
10 mins	Explore deeper	Individually	Exploring Guides
Small-group time			
10 mins	Snack break	Small groups	Workbench Leaders and Helpers
50 mins	Workbench exploration	Small groups	Workbench Leaders and Helpers
Together time			
5 mins	Finish up	All together	Presenters
AFTER CLUB			
10 mins	Team debrief and clearing up		All team

Restoration toolkit

Workshop basic list

Each Workshop contains a list of specific items needed for that Workshop's activities. The following list of items will be needed for each Workshop.

TEAM TIME
- ☐ Bibles

CLOCK IN
- ☐ registration forms
- ☐ consent forms
- ☐ collection slips
- ☐ registers
- ☐ Workbench allocation list
- ☐ pens
- ☐ sticky labels

WORKBENCH WELCOME
- ☐ scissors
- ☐ sticky tape
- ☐ colouring pens and pencils
- ☐ glue sticks
- ☐ a sign with the Workbench team name
- ☐ a large box for storing your group's materials and booklets
- ☐ copies of the Workbench shouts (pages 60 and 61)

THE RESTORATION STATION WORKOUT
- ☐ appropriate music with a good beat
- ☐ Setting the scene: two armchairs or smaller chairs

EXPLORE!
- ☐ a Bible
- ☐ the Bible verse to remember

EXPLORE DEEPER
- ☐ copies of the BIG questions

Talking
- ☐ beanbags or cushions

Creating
- ☐ A4 paper
- ☐ felt-tip pens
- ☐ scissors
- ☐ glue sticks
- ☐ pencils
- ☐ copies of the Workshop images

Thinking
- ☐ cushions or beanbags
- ☐ copies of the Workshop images

SNACK BREAK
- ☐ refreshments

WORKBENCH EXPLORATION
- ☐ copies of the *Toolbox* or *Logbook*, for each child
- ☐ pens and felt-tip pens or colouring pencils

PROGRAMME

THE TEAM
RECRUITING YOUR PERSONNEL

To run **The Restoration Station**, you'll need to recruit a team of willing and able volunteers who will take responsibility for various aspects of your programme. Everyone must be recruited in line with your organisation's recruitment and safeguarding policies.

You will also need to refer to the adult-to-child ratios as described in your safeguarding policy to determine how many volunteers you will need (remember that any young team members under the age of 18 count as children). You may find it helpful to set a limit on the number of children who can attend – determined by how many volunteers you are able to recruit. Alternatively, you may have a good idea of how many children and young people you are expecting to attend and recruit your team of leaders and helpers based on those numbers.

Of course, depending on the size of your holiday club, you may find that one person on your team can hold several roles at the same time. For example, as mentioned below, Exploring Guides could also be part of your Registration team.

Every team member should wear a badge that clearly identifies them and their role. Children should also wear name badges at all times. (Name badges should be removed at the end of **The Restoration Station** each day and kept securely at the venue.) Any adult or child seen not wearing an appropriate badge should be challenged.

You could choose to have some T-shirts printed for the team members, and ones in a different colour for the children.

Team roles

WORKBENCH LEADERS AND WORKBENCH HELPERS

Workbench Leaders and Helpers will work with the same Workbench team of children over the course of **The Restoration Station**. Workbench Leaders are those with overall responsibility for the children and young people in their group, and should be over 18. Workbench Helpers can be under 18 (but over the upper age limit for **The Restoration Station**). Under-18s must not take direct responsibility for the children in the Workbench team; when working out adult-to-child ratios for the club, they are counted as children. Workbench Helpers are there to assist Workbench Leaders and work alongside the children.

REGISTRATION TEAM

You will need several team members who can take responsibility for registering the children and young people on each day of your club. Ideally, they will have good people skills as they will be the first point of contact with the parents and children. Make sure the registration process is in line with your safeguarding policy and data protection policy. Although members of the Registration team may be able to fulfil other roles, they cannot be Workbench Leaders or Workbench Helpers as, once children are registered, they will need to be sent straight to their Workbench team table. The Registration team will also need to keep an accurate record of which team members attend each day, and which Leaders and Helpers are with each group.

PRESENTERS

One or two upfront Presenters lead the all-together time. These should be experienced adults who are confident when standing in front of a group of children. They will need to set the scene for each day and share the Bible story.

EXPLORING GUIDES

During 'Explore deeper', Exploring Guides are needed to work with each of the three groups. Guides in the Chatting area will need to facilitate a discussion based around the Workshop questions and any questions the children may have. Guides in the Creating area will need to help the children find the bits they need and offer general assistance. In the Thinking area, the Guide is there to gently enforce the quiet and direct the children to the images and questions. In all three areas, the Guides are simply there as facilitators and not for directing the children's exploring.

FIRST AID

You will need to ensure that you have at least one qualified first aider available at all times during your holiday club. Check your health and safety policy for advice on numbers of first aiders required at your event.

SAFEGUARDING

You will also need to ensure that every member of your team is aware of who will function as the Safeguarding Lead for **The Restoration Station**, and that all team members are trained appropriately, in accordance with your safeguarding policy.

DRAMA TEAM

Each day's drama requires two people. Chris the carpenter (male or female) is the main character and features every day. A different Bible character appears each day (preferably in biblical costume). The drama should be presented without scripts, if possible. The drama script can either be learned verbatim or ad-libbed from a list of bullet points. The presentation should be slick and well rehearsed – it is a significant part of the Bible input.

REFRESHMENTS TEAM

You will need a team to prepare refreshments ready to take them to each Workbench team table when it's time for 'Snack break'. This could possibly be done by Workbench Helpers if you don't have enough people for a separate team.

THE CHILDREN
EXPLORING THE BIBLE AND ENCOUNTERING JESUS

Getting to know the children

The Restoration Station provides a great opportunity to connect with children and help them explore the Bible and encounter Jesus. There are plenty of moments to talk with children, get to know them and ask questions. It's easy to think that all the spiritual input happens through the story and prayers, or from the upfront Presenters. However, those moments of conversation around the table, over making activities or during games can also be very meaningful.

The children will be allocated to a small Workbench team of up to ten children. This provides a great opportunity for Workbench Leaders and Workbench Helpers to develop appropriate, healthy and meaningful relationships with the children.

Often, when speaking with children it can be easy to stay on the safe topics – favourite sport, holiday destinations, and so on. **The Restoration Station** provides a prime opportunity to truly connect, go deeper and facilitate real thinking and reflection. Try to take those moments of conversation, wherever they are, to ask questions that open further discussion about life, God, Jesus, faith, church and more. Pray as a team of leaders and helpers for boldness and opportunities. Remember to encourage each other with stories of conversations during 'Team debrief' at the end of the session (making sure that, within the bounds of your safeguarding policy, you respect a child's rights not to have their thoughts and feelings shared more widely than appropriate).

Group dynamics can be tricky at a holiday club, especially if most of the children don't know each other, or if some know each other really well. The Workbench Leaders and Workbench Helpers will need to help quiet children to participate in ways that are appropriate for them, while making sure those who talk a lot allow others a chance to speak. A practical suggestion for dealing with talkative children might be to invite anyone who wants to say something to hold a themed object (a toy spanner or wrench would work well) and explain that they can only speak while they are holding the object. (If they are reluctant to pass it on to someone else who has something they want to say, you could put a time limit on each contribution!)

ASKING QUESTIONS

Make sure that the children don't feel bombarded by questions, but when you do ask them something, you could follow up with, 'Why?' Fight the urge to tell them the answer! This is about encouraging the children to explore. You could ask:

- What's most important to you?
- Do you think there is a God?
- If you do think there is a God, what do you think God is like?
- Who do you think Jesus is? Is he: not real, a good person, a teacher, God's Son?

Share something of who you are and what you believe, too. Keep it short, keep it simple, keep it child-friendly, keep it positive! Be aware that, as they get to know you, the children will want to please you and, as a result, may give you an answer they think you want to hear.

You might talk about:

- what your response to the above questions would be
- a short, appropriate story from your life, when God has helped you
- a time when God answered your prayer
- a time when God answered a prayer in a way you weren't expecting.

CHILDREN WITH ADDITIONAL NEEDS

The term 'additional needs' covers a wide spectrum of issues. Each child with additional needs coming to **The Restoration Station** will benefit hugely if you think through what will help them as an individual to get the best from it. Here are a few examples to help you consider what might need doing:

- Those with physical disabilities may need adaptations to certain activities, such as games, or the table at which they make things, or larger print for those with visual issues.
- Children with autism will benefit from being told each day what is happening in the programme, and may need a visual, printed schedule with verbal updates if last-minute changes are made.
- A child with learning disabilities may need to be in a younger age group if they can't cope with the level at which their peers are talking.
- A child in foster care might not need any special adaptations (apart from not appearing in any photographs of the activities) but would benefit from their Workbench Leader being aware (in confidence) of their circumstances.
- If you use a pre-booking system for children and become aware that a child with additional needs is coming, contact their parent or carer and ask what you can do to help them get the best out of **The Restoration Station**. Make sure you have enough team members to assign a one-to-one carer, if needed. If a child turns up on the day to register, make sure you have a conversation with the person who brings them about what extra help they might need, and check back with them during the week.

CHILDREN FROM OTHER FAITHS

Because the focus of this club is on children who are not from a church background, in one sense there is no need to make special provision for children of other faiths. But it will be important that you explain carefully certain truths about Jesus. Some faiths will respect him as a prophet but no more, while others will recognise numerous gods, not just one. Be honest and open in your publicity that **The Restoration Station** is a Christian event, so that any parent who sends their child knows they will hear Bible stories. Think ahead about the words you use, the things you ask children to do and the questions they might raise because of their experiences of another faith; be ready to respect their experience and belief. Avoid making sweeping statements or judgements about their faith. Pray for the Holy Spirit to work in them, as it is his role to convince them who Jesus is, not ours.

CHILDREN FROM A 5% BACKGROUND

If you have used a Scripture Union holiday club resource book before, you will be used to reading a paragraph about how to help children with no church background to get the best from the club. But as we are now focusing on those children (the 95), you will need to think briefly about the 5% or so of children in your community who do have a connection with church and may come to **The Restoration Station**. They may make up more than 5% of the children present, but you should still make everything appropriate and accessible to those with no church background.

Children from the 5% are probably comfortable coming to church and they will probably know the Bible stories used. On a practical note, they may be at the venue a long time before and after other children because their parent is involved on the team. So how can you help them to have a great time?

If you know the children well, it would be great to help them understand why there has been this shift of focus. In advance, explain the importance of giving children who don't come to church the opportunity to hear about Jesus. Ask them to pray for those who will come, and for God to work in their lives. Help them to think about some of the things they can do to make this work: inviting their friends to come to **The Restoration Station**, not always answering the questions immediately without giving others chance to think, listening to the stories without interrupting and saying they know what comes next (if they listen really carefully, they might learn something new!) and so on. Reassure them they will still enjoy it, and that you want and need them there. Encourage them to talk in their Workbench teams about what Jesus means to them. They can be peer evangelists! But they are still children, and may find it hard when they aren't allowed to shine with their Bible knowledge. Think carefully about whether it's better to spread the 5% children between Workbench teams, or to put them in a Workbench team together so they can focus on growing in their faith.

WORKBENCH TEAMS

The children at **The Restoration Station** should be divided into Workbench teams of up to ten children, each with a Workbench Leader and one or more Workbench Helpers.

Each Workbench team can be the name of a skilled craft worker who might contribute to a restoration process. The name of their trade should be on display and clearly visible to everyone. The children's name badges should also list their trade. For example: John Brown, Silversmith.

Assuming that each Workbench team will have a maximum of ten children, we have suggested eight teams, named as follows: Silversmiths; Woodturners; Stonemasons; Metalworkers; Sculptors; Potters; Blacksmiths; Tailors.

Each Workbench team performs a Workbench team 'shout' during Listen up! that describes their trade. These can be tricky to compose in a limited time, so we have some ready-made shouts! Feel free to adapt them, or create your own version from scratch. The shouts are available on pages 60 and 61, and also to download from su.org.uk/TheRestorationStation.

THE CHILDREN

Talking with children about healing and brokenness

When exploring big issues during your small-group time you may find that some children will ask poignant and challenging questions. This is a normal and healthy response to the topics raised, and should be handled in a positive and sensitive way.

You may feel ill-equipped to provide a 'neat' answer to such questions, which is absolutely fine!

A few things to remember:

- be honest in your responses
- be confident in what you say, even if that means saying that you are not sure
- be committed to exploring and discussing alongside the child – if you say that you'll come back to them after finding more information, make sure you do!

To help you consider how you might respond to the questions children ask, we have included a few suggestions below:

I don't have a broken leg, why do I need Jesus?

It's important to help children understand that Jesus didn't just come to heal broken bodies. His heart is to restore, to make all things new, back to how he always wanted them to be. We need Jesus to bring healing in all areas of our lives.

I'm not broken on the inside, why do I need Jesus?

Being 'broken' on the inside could point to a variety of emotional, mental and personal issues. Many (but by no means all!) children have yet to experience this kind of brokenness and some may even struggle to understand the concept. For those who don't feel they have anything for Jesus to 'fix', it's important to emphasise that Jesus wants to help us be the best version of ourselves and that Christians believe that it's only through knowing God that this can happen in its fullness.

I'm not sad and my life isn't difficult, why do I need Jesus?

Focusing on stories of healing and restoration may lead children to wonder what following Jesus looks like when life is good. It might be helpful to explain that Christians believe, whether things are going well or not so well, Jesus is there for us. He celebrates with us when we are happy, cheers us on when we are facing challenges and loves us unconditionally, whatever is happening and wherever we are.

Apart from healing people, what else did Jesus do/say while he was here on earth?

If time allows, you could share different stories from the Bible that illustrate the kinds of things Jesus said and did during his time on earth. If time is short, you could simply explain that as well as healing people, Jesus did many other miracles like calming a storm and feeding 5,000 people with a few loaves and fishes; he also told stories to help us understand who he is and how much God loves us.

Why did God send Jesus in the first place?

It's important to help children to see that Jesus is part of the big story of the Bible. That story starts with God making the world and everything in it, and ends with the world being restored to how God always intended it to be. You might find it helpful to summarise the 'big story' as follows: God made the world and everything in it and he was happy with everything he had made. God loved the people he had made and wanted them to live in friendship with him. One day the people decided to turn away from God. This broke God's heart and broke the people's relationship with God. God gave everything he had to restore that broken relationship, including his only Son, Jesus.

Why does Jesus heal some people and not others?

Children are particularly sensitive to issues of fairness and justice. As such, they are likely to be particularly disturbed to discover that Jesus heals some people, but not others. While Christians disagree on why this might be, there is broad agreement that healing in all its fullness will be present at the end of time and that between now and then, we will see glimpses of the complete restoration God is ultimately bringing about. When explaining this to the children in your group, acknowledge that this can be difficult to understand and focus on the fact that, even in our confusion and struggle, God is still with us through the Holy Spirit.

Why doesn't Jesus heal me/my family/my friends?

For children who have asked God for healing and have not seen the result they expected, it can seem as though God doesn't care, or perhaps that they are somehow undeserving of his love. It's important to explain that this is not the case. Children may find it helpful to know that even in the Bible itself there are occasions when Jesus didn't heal someone immediately when asked (Luke 8:40–56), and when Jesus prayed for the same person more than once (Mark 8:22–25).

Why did God let my friend/relative die?

For children dealing with the loss of a friend or a relative, anger at God for letting this happen is a normal response. It can be helpful for children to hear that you understand how sad it is when someone we know dies, and that Jesus understands the sadness we feel. Reassure the children in your group that while we don't always understand why God doesn't intervene to prevent the death of someone we love, we can hold on to his promise to be with us in our pain and ultimately wipe every tear from our eyes (Revelation 21:1–4).

Why doesn't God take away pain?

Dealing with pain can be particularly difficult for younger children, especially when they hear that God can take away our pain but doesn't always do so. Helping children to understand the causes of pain and the complex relationship between sin, suffering and free will is not easy, but it's important to acknowledge that pain is part of the broken world we live in. Bringing children back to God's ultimate plan to restore our broken world can be a helpful focus, but only when it is balanced with his heart of love and compassion for the pain we continue to experience.

> Responding to these kinds of questions may well raise even more questions for children who have little or no knowledge of Christianity. If this happens, you might want to consider finding a way to record the questions the children have and use these as a basis for some follow-on sessions or activities after your holiday club has finished.

SETTING UP
PREPARING THE SPACE

The time you ask your team to arrive before each session begins will depend on how much preparation you expect to do prior to the children arriving. If you have decorated your venue in advance (and are able to leave it decorated for the duration of your club) you will have less daily preparation to do. If you are not able to decorate in advance, your daily preparation time will be longer.

Station areas

REGISTRATION AND COLLECTION

The registration area – also the point where parents wait to collect their children at the end of each session – would most logically be placed near the entrance to your venue.

If possible, encourage parents and carers to complete booking forms in advance of **The Restoration Station** holiday club. These should then be returned to the leader of **The Restoration Station**, the school office or the community group leader, depending on how you make contact with families. This means you can allocate children to Workbench teams in advance, and you will already be aware of any dietary requirements, medical issues and physical, educational or behavioural needs. Remember to check these when planning your activities and allocating team members.

In some contexts pre-registering is not practical, so you will need to ensure that you have plenty of volunteers who are able to help greet the children and their parents or carers each session, providing them with the registration form to fill in. *Children should not attend the event unless written permission has been given.*

If you are able to set up an area for those already registered and an additional area for those who need to register on the day, this will help to avoid long queues before the day begins. Make sure that, when the registration desk closes, all forms are moved to a safe place where they can be accessed easily if needed by designated team members, and not by any parents leaving late or arriving early.

Make sure all data is collected in accordance with your organisation's GDPR policy.

Registration can be a lengthy process, so you might choose to open your doors earlier for the first session. On subsequent days you may want to adapt your registration process so those who registered previously are fast-tracked, while making space for any new children to be registered. You will need to keep accurate lists of who is in which Workbench team, in case of fire or other emergencies, and especially if you should need to evacuate the building. Each Workbench Leader should have an up-to-date list of who is in their team. Make sure you have a clear plan of what you would do in case of an emergency, and where the children would gather outside. The main upfront presenter(s) should explain this to the children at the beginning of every session. Keep this clear but low-key, so as not to worry the children.

UPFRONT AREA

You will need an area where the upfront Presenter(s) will be when leading 'Listen up!', 'Explore!' and 'Finish up'.

There needs to be a floor space from which all the children attending **The Restoration Station** will be able to see and hear everything that is happening. As it is also the area where the drama will take place, it can be decorated as if it is a workshop. Be creative and invite people to lend appropriate and safe tools and equipment that can be displayed, or perhaps you could use some toy versions instead of real tools. You could also use bigger items, such as stepladders, boxes, rolls of fabric… whatever you can find! (The BBC programme *The Repair Shop* may give you some good ideas!)

WORKBENCH TEAM AREAS

Each team will sit at a named Workbench team table, possibly placed around the edge of the room. Basically, you need one long table (or two arranged end to end) with seating for each child arranged around the table(s). Although having the children sitting around a table takes up space, it will help them to feel part of the team and also to focus on the various activities, and it will be easier for them to write and draw in their Restoration notebooks. If you have ten children per Workbench team, you could seat four children either side and one at each end.

You could decorate the Workbenches with items relating to each team, eg decorations for the Tailors' Workbench could include rolls of fabric and tape measures.

The children will be eating and drinking refreshments at the tables during 'Snack break', so keep this in mind when choosing and arranging decorations.

EXPLORE DEEPER AREAS

During 'Explore deeper' you will need three specific areas. Depending on your space, you should prepare your 'Explore deeper' areas in advance – this could be full set-up of each dedicated space, or it could be preparing a box that can be quickly unpacked into a multi-use space at the appropriate time.

Talking

The Talking area would benefit from some floor cushions or low chairs where children and leaders can chat together easily. If you are expecting a large number of children, you may want to set up several smaller circles of cushions or chairs in your talking area so that everyone gets a chance to speak.

Creating

The Creating area will include the use of colouring pens and modelling materials; it would benefit from having tables, if possible, or perhaps a large plastic sheet on the floor.

Thinking

The Thinking area is a space set up away from the noise and chatter of the other groups. It would benefit from some floor cushions, beanbags or low chairs.

RESOURCES
ADDITIONAL OPTIONS AND ADVICE

ADDITIONAL WORKSHOPS

This holiday club resource book contains three half-day sessions that will form a complete three-day holiday club. For those who wish to run a four- or five-day club, two additional half-day sessions are available at su.org.uk/TheRestorationStation.

Each session works independently of the others, but care will need to be taken to ensure that the children understand the context of the story they are exploring in terms of the overarching narrative around Jesus' life.

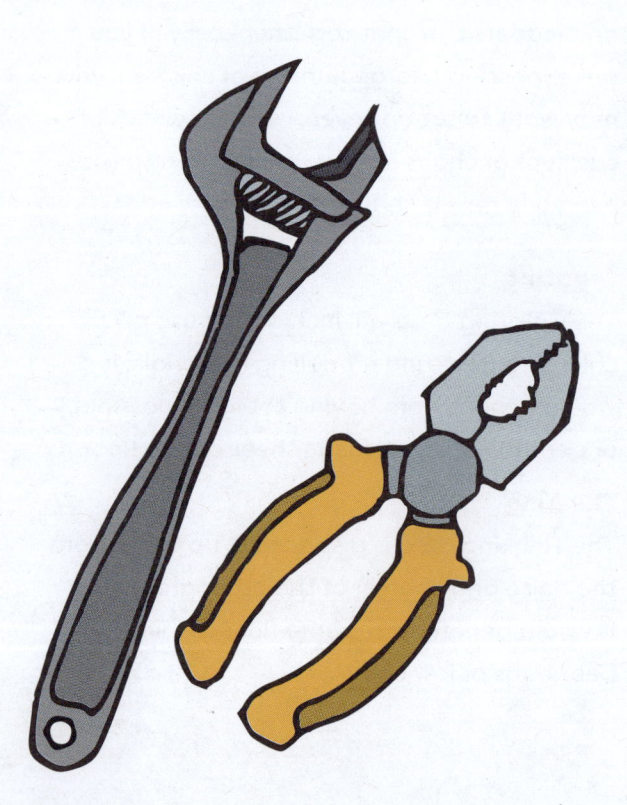

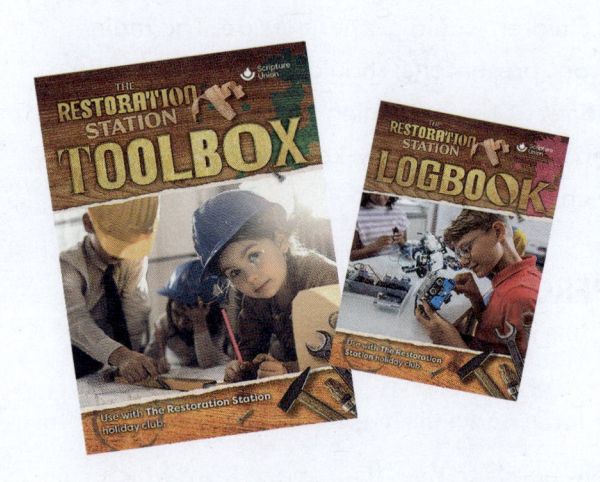

BOOKLETS FOR CHILDREN

Toolbox
For younger children

This 32-page booklet contains selected Bible text taken from the Contemporary English Version, along with small-group material, puzzles and activities, for younger children.

Logbook
For older children

This 48-page booklet contains all the key Bible text taken from the Contemporary English Version, along with small-group material, puzzles and activities. It is ideal for use with 8 to 11s.

DRAMA SCRIPTS

Short drama scripts for Workshops 1 to 3, featuring Chris the carpenter and a character from the Bible story, are included in this resource book, but are also available as a separate download. Drama scripts for Additional Workshops A and B are available to download from su.org.uk/TheRestorationStation.

DAISY AND DAN ANIMATIONS

Stories of healing and restoration can raise some big questions for children as they look at brokenness in the world around them and, possibly, in their own family situations. An animation featuring the characters Daisy and Dan, designed to help to explore how Jesus can be present in those situations, is available for each Workshop from su.org.uk/TheRestorationStation. The article 'Talking with children about healing and brokeness', on pages 22 and 23, offers extra guidance on this potentially difficult topic.

PUBLICITY

See the inside back cover for details of **The Restoration Station** holiday club publicity materials produced by Christian Publicity and Outreach. (Please note, CPO resources are not available through Scripture Union.)

OTHER DOWNLOADABLE RESOURCES

A range of downloads to help you run your club is available from su.org.uk/TheRestorationStation, including:

- printable versions of the photocopiable resources
- team roles
- Explore deeper BIG questions
- Workshop images
- logos
- poster
- club aims form
- evaluation form
- and lots more!

LEGAL REQUIREMENTS AND SAFEGUARDING

There are various legal requirements you will need to be familiar with and conform to as you prepare for your holiday club. Things to consider include:

- safeguarding and child protection policies
- safer recruitment policies and procedures
- provision of adequate space(s) in your venue
- meeting adult-to-child ratios
- registering your club with any necessary authorities
- insurance
- data protection
- accidents and first aid
- issues of health and safety, including risk assessments
- fire procedures and guidelines
- food hygiene.

To obtain up-to-date information please check with the relevant authorities.

FOLLOW UP
AN ONGOING STRATEGY

What next?

You may think this is a strange place to put a section about follow-up to **The Restoration Station**. However, the whole event will be far more effective if it's part of an ongoing strategy of work with children from the 95, rather than just a once-a-year event. If **The Restoration Station** helps you to connect with children who don't come to church, make sure you have some event or activity planned to take place not too long after it ends, so that you can build on these connections.

It would be great if you could have something happening within a few weeks, before you've forgotten the children's names. It doesn't have to be a massive event: you could hold a games and pizza party or a family activity afternoon. If it's planned in advance and you have decided on the type of activity and the date and time, you can distribute invitations at **The Restoration Station**.

You could maximise the opportunities you've created by running events regularly through the year. It might even be that you do just one session of **The Restoration Station** once a month, spreading it over five months.

Having a 'What's next?' approach means there will always be something on offer for people to look forward to. Events you organise could tie in with special occasions through the year, such as Valentine's Day, Mothering Sunday, Pancake Day, Easter, Father's Day, Harvest, All Saints' Day and so on. Offering personal invitations and tickets to these events means that people are more likely to turn up, even if a ticket isn't strictly necessary! As children (and perhaps their families, too?) come to things on offer, you'll need to think about how you take them on from that first connection, to the next step.

You may decide to run a regular club as a follow-on from **The Restoration Station**. It doesn't have to happen every week: regular could mean once a month, or the first and third Tuesday evening or Saturday morning, for example. You could run weekly clubs for half a term, such as six weeks after October half term through to Christmas, and then from February half term towards Easter, for another six weeks. You may find it easier to recruit team members to help you if it's for a limited time: many people are, quite understandably, reluctant to commit to something indefinitely. The same is probably true for parents who have to organise busy lives and get their children to and from activities!

It may be that, as you plan and prepare for **The Restoration Station**, you can have others planning a programme for what follows. For example, if your church is large enough, don't feel you and your team have to do everything. Invite others to be part of this exciting journey!

Faith journeys

Now we're going to think about follow-up from the children's perspective, taking into account the need to not just maintain contact, but to help them move on in their journey towards, or with, Jesus.

What each child needs to continue in their journey will vary. **The Restoration Station** may have given some children initial understanding, so they can appreciate a bit of the big picture, but there is a lot more to see before they are ready to decide who Jesus is, never mind consider whether they should follow him.

Others will have worked out that Jesus is God's Son. They might need to explore a little more, but also be helped to think about the 'so what?' that follows knowing who Jesus is.

For some, the response will simply be wanting to know more. Others will want to hold on to the positives of **The Restoration Station**. Some may want to make a commitment to follow Jesus. It's important to allow the children to respond in their own way and at their own pace. To find out more about how you can walk alongside children as they explore who Jesus is, consider their response to him and, hopefully, go on to help them grow a vibrant, personal faith in Jesus, contact your local Scripture Union Mission Enabler through www.scriptureunion.org.uk.

30

THE WORK SHOPS

WORKSHOP 1
Jesus meets a very important man

BIBLE PASSAGE: JOHN 4:46-53

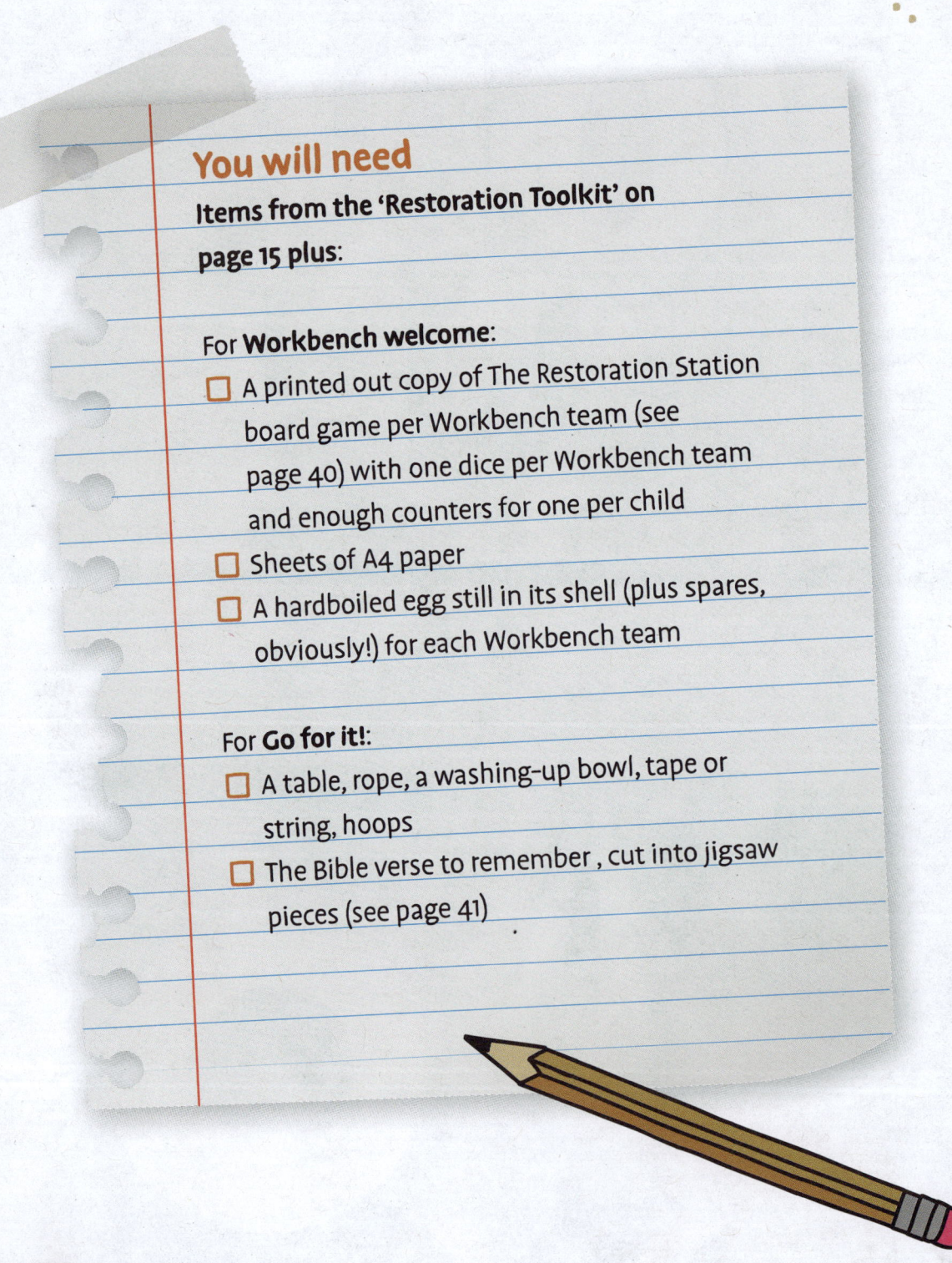

You will need

Items from the 'Restoration Toolkit' on page 15 plus:

For **Workbench welcome**:
- [ ] A printed out copy of The Restoration Station board game per Workbench team (see page 40) with one dice per Workbench team and enough counters for one per child
- [ ] Sheets of A4 paper
- [ ] A hardboiled egg still in its shell (plus spares, obviously!) for each Workbench team

For **Go for it!**:
- [ ] A table, rope, a washing-up bowl, tape or string, hoops
- [ ] The Bible verse to remember, cut into jigsaw pieces (see page 41)

Workshop 1 schedule

TEAM TIME
(30 minutes)

Invite your whole team to gather together before registration begins. This should not be a time for setting up your venue or completing last-minute preparations, rather a time to pause, reflect and pray together.

Read the Bible story for the session (John 4:46–53, Jesus healing the official's son). Remind everyone that **The Restoration Station** emphasises Jesus' power to heal and restore, and this is exactly what Jesus did.

Run through the programme for the session and check that everyone knows what they are doing.

Pray for one another and for the activities, the children and God's work in everyone.

When it's time to open the doors, have some upbeat Christian music playing quietly in the background and make sure the team members are in position, ready to give the children a warm welcome to **The Restoration Station**.

CLOCK-IN
(10 minutes)

As each child arrives, make sure your registration team is ready to greet them. If you were able to obtain registration and consent forms in advance, you will simply need to check off each child as they arrive and double-check the arrangements for collection.

If the children attending **The Restoration Station** have not been pre-registered, you will need to ensure you have the space for parents and carers to complete the relevant paperwork and a team member to attend to them. No child should attend the club without permission.

Once each child is registered, give them their name badge with their skill listed on it (for example, John Brown, Silversmith). If possible, have a team member take them to their Workbench table. (If not, make it very clear where they need to go.) When registration is completed, remember that each Workbench Leader will need a list of the children in their Workbench team (along with any food allergy information), in case of emergency.

WORKBENCH WELCOME
(20 minutes)

Make sure each child feels very welcome when they arrive at their Workbench team table. Show them where they can sit. Explain to all the children what their particular trade is and then invite them to join in with **The Restoration Station** board game in the middle of the table. When they land on a square with a question, invite them to answer it. While they are playing, use their names as much as possible, with a sneaky glance at their name badges, if necessary!

Allow up to 12 minutes for playing. After that time, if the game has not finished, ask a Workbench Helper to make a note of where each child's counter is on the board, then put it to one side, ready to use again if there is time later in the session, or tomorrow. It's important to do the second activity, as it sets the scene for the Bible story.

Challenge the children to see which tasks they can do from the following list:

- Can they wiggle their ears?
- Can they touch their ear with their elbow?
- Can they fold a sheet of A4 paper in half eight times?
- Can they get the creases out of the paper they just folded?
- Can they break an egg by holding it with one finger at the top of the egg and their thumb at the bottom of the egg (not the side), and squeezing as hard as they can? (Use the hard-boiled eggs for this.)

Explain that, apart from number 1, these tasks are impossible! Say that, later on, they are going to hear a true story from the Bible, about something seemingly impossible that did actually happen!

LISTEN UP!
(10 minutes)

The Presenters should introduce themselves and welcome the children to **The Restoration Station**. They mention essentials, such as where the toilets are, where the fire exits are and what to do in an emergency (keeping it very calm and relatively low-key, so the children are not worried).

Next, they explain that **The Restoration Station** is a place where anything that is spoiled or broken can be repaired and restored, and, to do that, there are lots of very skilled people who work hard to make that happen. They point out each Workbench team around the room, with a brief explanation of what each trade is all about. They then tell the children they have 5 minutes in their Workbench team to practise the Workbench shout, which their Workbench Leaders and Workbench Helpers will teach them (they don't necessarily need to learn it as it is printed for them to read).

After 5 minutes, the Presenters go round the room and listen to each Workbench team as they do their shout, making an encouraging comment after each one.

Finally, they ask the children about the impossible tasks they tried to do in their Workbench team. Could the children do any of them?

THE RESTORATION STATION WORKOUT
(5 minutes)

One of the Presenters tells the children that now is the time to get some exercise. They invite the children to do some simple exercises, such as star jumps, running on the spot and so on. If you have any children with physical limitations, the Presenter should include appropriate moves that they will be able to join in with, perhaps with assistance. Make sure that, if you have music, it is upbeat. The Presenter should be enthusiastic and encourage everyone to join in, but be aware that some children may just prefer to watch, and that's OK. When it is finished, the Presenter should invite the children to sit down ready to Explore! the story.

EXPLORE!
(20 minutes)

One of the Presenters asks the children what would happen if one morning, when they woke up, they felt really unwell. Would they go to school? Why not? What might happen next? (The children may give answers along the lines of staying in bed, having some medicine and so on.) They then ask if whoever cares for them at home has ever had to phone the doctor for advice or make an appointment to go to the doctor's surgery.

The Presenter says that, probably, if they saw the doctor, he or she might have looked in their ears with a special tool, and asked them to open their mouth and say, 'Aaaah' so they could see their throat. Perhaps the doctor would have felt their neck, and maybe their tummy, too. Then the doctor might have said, 'Keep taking the medicine until you feel better.' Or, they might have told them that they needed some antibiotics, and given them a prescription to take to the chemist. The antibiotics may have taken a bit of time to work, but they probably had begun to feel better after a few days and, eventually, had been able to go back to school.

The Presenter then asks the children, 'Do you think the doctor would ever just say, "Don't worry. You're better NOW!"?' They point out that that doesn't happen. Doctors are very clever, but they can't heal people just like that. It's impossible. No one can do that, especially if they are somewhere else – like on the end of the phone. It's just not possible. Or… is it?

Holding up a Bible, the Presenter explains the children are going to listen to a true story from this very special book, called the Bible. They explain that Christians believe that the Bible tells us true stories about God and how he created the world and people, and that it also tells us about one very special man, called Jesus. (If it's necessary or appropriate to do so, you could say to the children that they may have heard of Jesus, even if they don't know much about him.)

The Presenter tells the children that, in this story, they will hear how Jesus met someone called 'an official'. Basically, an official is a very important person.

The Presenter, or another member of the team who is a confident reader, reads John 4:46–54 from the Contemporary English Version. (It would be good to read from the Bible that the Presenter shows the children, so that they are reinforcing where the story is coming from.) Make sure the reader has practised it in advance and that they read it slowly and clearly, but also make it sound exciting! They should ask the children to listen carefully for not just one, but two impossible things that Jesus did.

After the story has been read, the Presenter asks the children to put up their hand if they can tell you one or both of the impossible things that Jesus did. (*He turned water into wine and healed the boy immediately, from a distance!*)

After listening to the children's answers (and making sure they have found the two impossible things), the Presenter stands aside to let Chris the carpenter introduce herself or himself and perform the drama 'Meet the official' (from pages 38 and 39).

When the drama has finished, one of the Presenters introduces and plays the Daisy and Dan animation 'The Rock'. Before playing the animation, the Presenter explains that it is about two children called Daisy and Dan. Dan is worried about going back to school after a fight with a friend, Daisy shares how God can be our rock when we are worried.

EXPLORE DEEPER!
(5–10 minutes)

The Presenters offer the children some questions to help them think more about what they have just seen and heard. They explain the three different ways of exploring the questions and invite the children to choose which exploration area they want to go to: Talking; Creating; Thinking. It is important to make this a free choice – the children can choose whichever approach suits them best.

Today's BIG questions (available to download from su.org.uk/TheRestorationStation) are:

- What did the official ask Jesus to do?
- What did Jesus actually do?
- What would you have felt if you had been the official?
- Who do you run to when you are scared?

Talking

Talk with the children about the story and the questions. You may need to ask a question to get them started, and steer them back to the questions if they go off track, but encourage the children to do most of the talking. Try not to stifle the children's responses, particularly if their ideas are misguided. Gently and sensitively share your own thoughts and responses with the children, helping them to understand a view that differs from their own. Allow thought and imagination to flow, and ask more questions when a child answers a question. Help them to explore God's Word for themselves!

Creating

Provide the children with artist and making materials, and the Workshop 1 images (available to download), and encourage them to explore what they have heard, and the questions asked, in a creative way. This is a completely unguided activity – offer whatever help is asked for, but allow the children to create their own response.

Thinking

Have a space set up away from the noise and chatter of the other groups, where children can choose to think quietly and reflect on everything they have seen and heard. Provide copies of the questions and also the Workshop 1 images (available to download). You could provide some floor cushions, beanbags or other soft seating, and maybe some soft lighting. Make sure this space is far enough away from the talking so that children who prefer to reflect quietly can do so. Leaders in the thinking area should remind the children that they can talk with their Workbench Leader about what they have been reflecting on during the 'Explore Deeper!' time.

SNACK BREAK
(10 minutes)

When the time is up, the Presenters invite the children to return to their Workbench tables where Workbench Helpers will serve the refreshments.

TEAM EXPLORATION
(50 minutes)

The children stay in their Workbench teams for this section. Half the teams should start with 'Go for it!' while the other half start with 'Restoration information'. After about 20 minutes, swap the teams over (allowing up to 10 minutes for the swap to take place). Make sure everyone knows at the beginning that they will get a chance to do everything!

Go for it!
(20 minutes)

Ideally, play these games outside, but both could be played indoors if that's not possible. Bearing in mind what is most appropriate for your venue, the number of children you have and what can be achieved in 20 minutes, do one or both of the games outlined.

1. **Obstacle course**

In advance, set up a simple obstacle course to illustrate the official's journey, with a 'bridge' (table) to crawl under, 'gates' to jump over (rope laid on the ground), a 'hill' to climb (a zigzag path, marked out with string), a 'stream' to cross (a rectangular washing-up bowl of water) and a 'tunnel' to go through (a hoop for the children to put over their head and step out of).

Make sure you do a risk assessment in advance. Have Workbench Leaders and Workbench Helpers stationed at each obstacle to help any children who need it, but leave at least one Leader with each Workbench team.

Explain that the official in the story travelled quite a long way to find Jesus, and show them his journey in the form of the obstacle course. Invite the children to retrace his steps. Depending on the number of children, it could be a race, they could do it in pairs or it could be a timed activity. If possible, keep up a running commentary!

2. **Relay race**

Have a copy of the Bible verse from page 41 for each Workbench team, cut into 20 separate jigsaw pieces.

(Ideally, this should be enlarged; individual large jigsaw pieces are available to download from su.org.uk/TheRestorationStation.) The verse is 2 Corinthians 5:17: 'Anyone who belongs to Jesus has become a new person. The old life is gone; a new life has begun!'

Place the pieces on the ground at one end of the room or outside space. Ask each Workbench team to line up opposite them, one behind the other and about 15 paces away. On 'Go!' encourage the first child in the line to run and collect one piece and return to the Workbench team, going to the back of the line. Invite the next child to run and collect another jigsaw piece, and so on. When all the pieces have been collected, challenge the children to complete the jigsaw on the floor. (Some children find it hard to participate in relay races and don't always get it, so be ready to help them and perhaps have a practice run.) When the jigsaw is completed, invite everyone to gather around it on display on the floor and say the verse together, several times, helping those who still struggle to read.

Restoration information
(20 minutes)

Give each child a copy of the *Toolbox* (younger children) or *Logbook* (older children). Invite them to spend some time completing pages 5 to 8 (*Toolbox*) or pages 6 to 13 (*Logbook*) as they reflect on all that they have discovered today.

Depending on the children in your group, you could recap the story together, or even read it out again. Answer any questions they may have, looking at the Bible verses together and chatting about what the answer might be. In this way you can help the children to explore the Bible for themselves. Talk with the children about how it was immediate and complete healing. The boy was restored to full health by Jesus, even though Jesus was a very long way away! Ask them what they think about that.

Ask the children what they were thinking about during the 'Explore Deeper!' time and chat with them about this as they work on their booklets. For children wrestling with the idea of Jesus as healer, revisit the themes drawn out of the Daisy and Dan animation. Invite them to consider:
- What things might we feel in our bodies when we are worried? (Eg butterflies in our tummy; dizzy; shaky.)
- When we say to someone that they are 'a rock', what do we mean? (Reliable; dependable; strong; solid; unchanging.)
- Christians believe God is like 'a rock' in their lives. How do you feel about this idea?

Allow plenty of time for them to work through the booklet on their own, helping them if they wish.

FINISH UP
(5 minutes)

The Presenters wind up the session. They explain that, because Jesus can do anything – even impossible things – he can hear us when we talk to him. They say that we can do that aloud, or silently in our heads. Talking to Jesus and listening to what he says is called 'praying', or 'prayer'. (Depending on your context, it may helpful to briefly explain that Christians believe Jesus is still alive today, even though we can't see him here on earth.) The Presenters tell the children that they will say a 'Thank you' prayer to Jesus now, for the things we've learned and the fun we've had. They encourage the children to listen quietly and carefully and, if they want to agree and make it their prayer too, saying 'Amen' (which means 'I agree') at the end.

TEAM DEBRIEF
(10 minutes)

Before you start to clear up, pause together as a team and take time to reflect and evaluate the session. What worked well? Did anything not work well? What signs have you seen of God at work? How has God answered your prayers from earlier? Pray again for the children and the conversations they will be having at home.

THE WONDERFUL WORLD-FAMOUS WALK-IN WORKSHOP!

WORKSHOP DRAMA 1

Meet the official!

This can be performed as it is written (preferably without scripts!). Alternatively, it could also be an ad-lib drama, making sure the important points about restoration are made. Either way, it must be rehearsed in advance as good presentation is essential! It is performed in the 'Listen up!' area, which is already decorated as a workshop.

The characters

- **Chris the carpenter** (the name can be male or female)
- **Official** (biblical costume would be good, but isn't essential)

The props

- **Hard hat** (plus a pencil for behind an ear!)
- **Toy toolkit** (a bag or box labelled 'Toolkit', containing a hammer, a saw and a pot labelled 'Glue')
- **Large sign** on display: 'The Wonderful World-famous Walk-in Workshop'

A list of main points for ad-libbing Drama 1

If the drama is going to be ad-libbed, read through the main script when you rehearse, so that you get the feel of the plot.

Chris:
- Introduce yourself as Chris the carpenter
- Children guess – builder, carpenter, repairer

Official:
- Lost! Where am I? (Seem very confused!)

Chris:
- The Wonderful World-famous Walk-in Workshop! (Encourage the children to join in.)

Official:
- Who are you?
- I've just been speaking to a carpenter called Jesus!

Chris:
- Jesus is awesome!

Official:
- He healed my son, just like that, and my son wasn't even there!

Chris:
- Because Jesus is God's Son he can do the impossible!

Official:
- I need to go back to Bible times now
- I'll leave you to your restoring… I guess that's what Jesus does with people!

Chris:
- Absolutely!

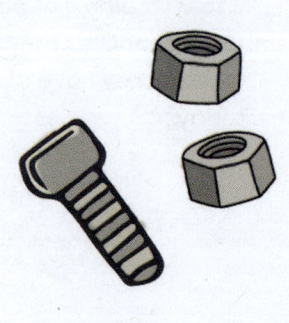

The script

Chris: (*Enter Chris, wearing a hard hat, holding a toolkit in one hand.*) Hi! I'm Chris. I'm really excited because I've just started a new job! (*Hold up toolkit. Put toolkit down and open it. Hold up a hammer in one hand, and a saw in the other.*) I could be a builder because I have a hammer (*hold up hammer*) and a saw (*hold up saw*). (*Pause, and look at each tool in turn.*) Or… I could be a carpenter, making things from wood.

But I also have glue (*hold up*), so I could be a furniture repairer – that's someone who mends things that are broken and makes them like new again. Can you guess which of those jobs I have now? Let's take a vote! (*Put tools down.*)

So… after I've counted to three, put your hand up if you think I'm a builder. Nod if you think I'm a carpenter. Wave if you think I'm a repairer. (*Demonstrate actions.*) Ready? One, two, three!

Well, actually, I'm all of those things! Can you put your hand up while you are nodding and wave at the same time, or is that impossible, I wonder? (*Demonstrate again.*) It is quite difficult, so well done! You can stop now!

Official: (*Enter, looking confused.*) Hello? Hello?

Chris: Hi!

Official: Oh hello! Can you help me? I'm lost. Well… sort of lost. I was just on my way home when, suddenly, I found myself (*pause and look around, frowning*) … here! Where am I?

Chris: You're at The Wonderful World-famous Walk-in Workshop!

Official: (*Look confused and scratch head.*) The what?

Chris: (*Encourage everyone to join in and say it with you.*) The Wonderful World-famous Walk-in Workshop! (*Point to sign.*) It's a workshop, where I mend things that are spoiled, or damaged, or broken. I restore them until they're like new again.

Official: So… who are you?

Chris: Most people call me Chris the carpenter, but I'm a builder and a repairer as well.

Official: I've just been speaking to a man who's a carpenter! His name is Jesus!

Chris: Oh, I know about Jesus! He's awesome! He does things that no one else can do.

Official: Tell me about it! He's healed my son and made him better – just like that (*click fingers*) – and my son wasn't even there (*sound incredulous*)! All Jesus did was say that it would happen, and it did, exactly when he said it would. How could he do that? It's impossible, but he did it!

Chris: Because he's Jesus. He's God's Son and he has God's amazing power. He can do anything! He can even do things that are impossible. That's how he healed your son and changed him back to the way he should be – not poorly or unwell any more.

Official: Well, thanks for welcoming me to The Wonderful World-famous Walk-in Workshop. I'd better get back to Bible times now and leave you to restoring things and making them like new. (*Pause, then say as if it has just occurred to you.*) I guess that's what Jesus does with people!

Chris: Absolutely! (*Both freeze.*)

WORKSHOP 1
PHOTOCOPIABLE PAGE

Board game

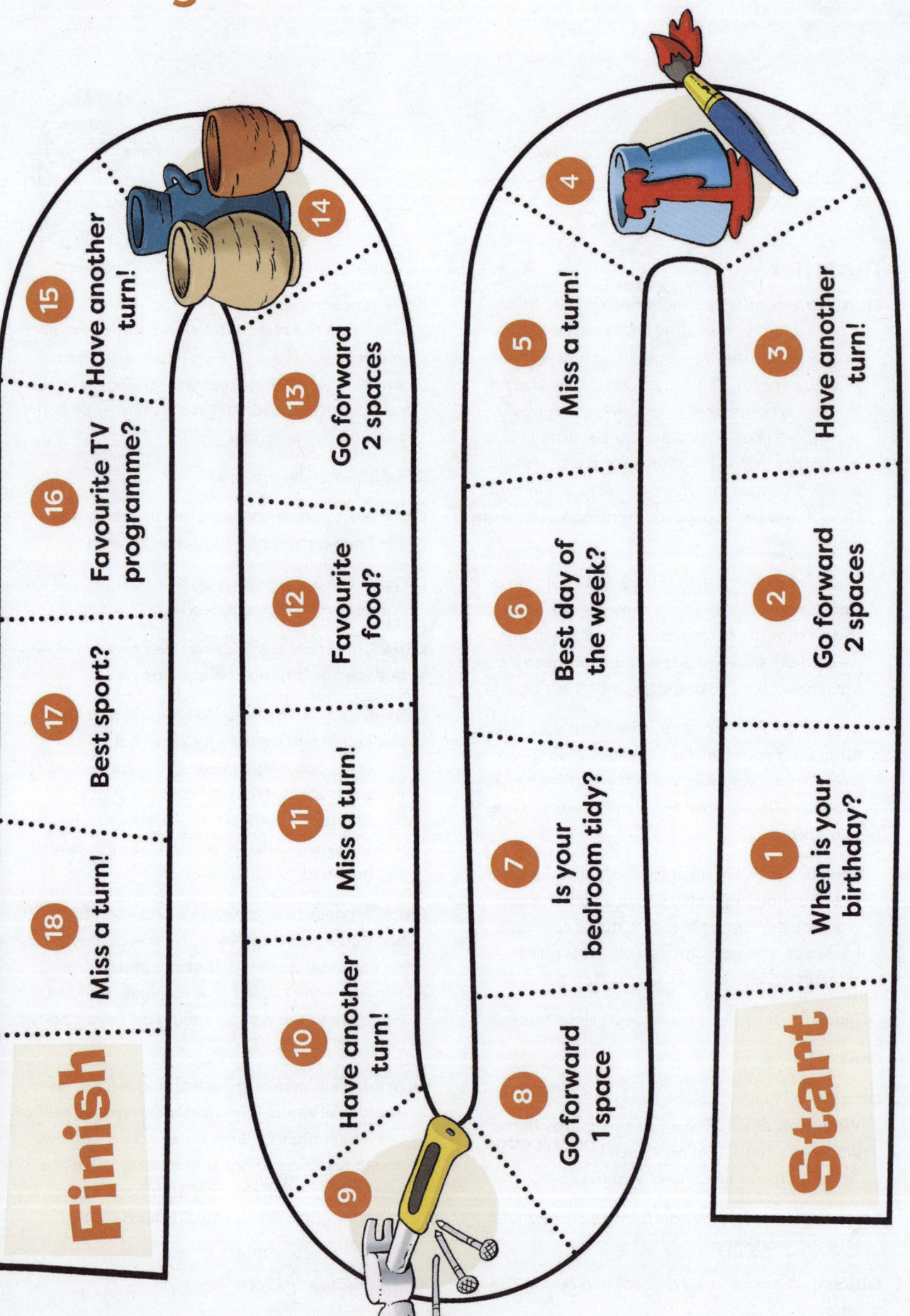

Start

1. When is your birthday?
2. Go forward 2 spaces
3. Have another turn!
4.
5. Miss a turn!
6. Best day of the week?
7. Is your bedroom tidy?
8. Go forward 1 space
9.
10. Have another turn!
11. Miss a turn!
12. Favourite food?
13. Go forward 2 spaces
14.
15.
16. Favourite TV programme?
17. Best sport?
18. Miss a turn!

Finish

40

Bible verse jigsaw

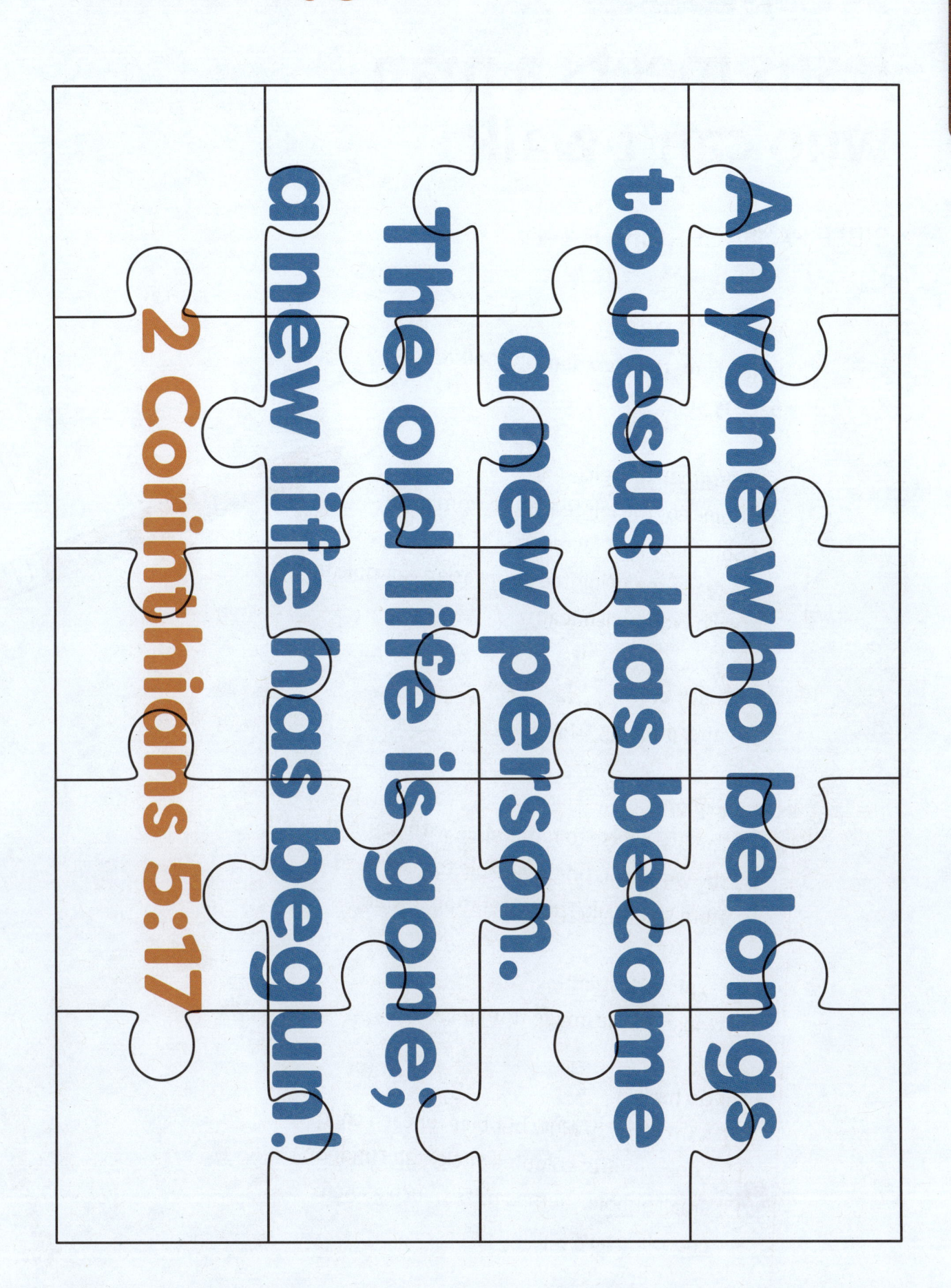

Anyone who belongs to Jesus has become a new person. The old life is gone; a new life has begun!

2 Corinthians 5:17

WORKSHOP 2
Jesus meets a man who can't walk

BIBLE PASSAGE: John 5:1–13

You will need

Items from the 'Restoration Toolkit' on page 15 plus:

For **Workbench welcome**:
- ☐ Copies of the jointed figure from page 50
- ☐ Split-pin paper fasteners
- ☐ A ready-made jointed figure as an example for each Workbench team

For **Snack break**:
- ☐ Paper drinking straws

For **Explore!**:
- ☐ The Bible verse to remember, with some of the words missing, available to download from su.org.uk/TheRestorationStation

For **Explore deeper!**:
- ☐ Copies of the image from page 51

For **Go for it!**:
- ☐ A small pot of blow bubbles for each child
- ☐ Cones, rope or coloured sticky tape (indoors)
- ☐ Small bubble-themed prizes, such as Aero chocolate bars (optional)

Workshop 2 schedule

TEAM TIME
(30 minutes)

Start by thanking everyone for their hard work in the first session and mention one or two encouraging things that happened. Read the Bible story for this session (John 5:1–13, Jesus healing the lame man). Say that, again, this is an amazing example of Jesus' power to restore someone in need and give them new life.

If you have any children attending The Restoration Station who have physical limitations or are disabled and possibly in a wheelchair, you will need to handle this story about a lame man very carefully and sensitively. If appropriate, it might be a good idea to chat with their parents or carers in advance. Discuss with the team the way you have decided to approach the story.

Run through the making activity with Workbench Leaders and Workbench Helpers – making a jointed man to represent the man in the story. Each Workbench team should have a ready-made man as an example. Remind the Workbench Leaders and Workbench Helpers that the children may need help with cutting out and making holes for the split-pin paper fasteners, and using the fasteners without cutting their fingers.

Pray for one another and for the day's activities, the children and God's work in everyone.

When it's time to open the doors, have some upbeat Christian music playing quietly in the background and make sure the team members are in position, ready to welcome the children back to **The Restoration Station**.

CLOCK-IN
(10 minutes)

As each child arrives, make sure your registration team is ready to welcome them.

Check in those who came yesterday, give parents and carers collection slips and provide name labels for the children.

Have registration forms available to register new children (remember that no child should attend the club without permission from their parent or carer).

When registration ends, take the registers to each Workbench Leader, so that they have them in case of fire or other emergency.

WORKBENCH WELCOME
(20 minutes)

As each child arrives, greet them by name; welcome any who are new. Explain that they are going to make a jointed figure who will be used in 'Explore!' later on, when they will hear another true story from the Bible. Show the children how to make their figure, and make sure each child puts their name on the back of their own figure.

While the children are making their jointed figures, ask the children what they can remember about the story of Jesus meeting a very important man.

Remind everyone of the name of your Workbench and do your Workbench shout together a few times.

LISTEN UP!
(10 minutes)

The Presenters introduce themselves again (there may be new children) and welcome everyone back to **The Restoration Station**. They remind the children that **The Restoration Station** is a place where anything that is spoiled or broken can be repaired and restored.

The Presenters pause and ask: 'Where are all the skilled workers?' They invite each Workbench team as they do their shout and, as before, make an encouraging comment about each one.

THE RESTORATION STATION WORKOUT
(5 minutes)

One of the Presenters tells the children that now is the time to get some exercise. They invite the children to do some simple exercises, such as star jumps, running on the spot and so on. If you have any children with physical limitations, the Presenter should include appropriate moves that they will be able to join in with, perhaps with assistance. Make sure that, if you have music, it is upbeat. The Presenter should be enthusiastic and encourage everyone to join in, but be aware that some children may just prefer to watch, and that's OK. When it is finished, the Presenter should invite the children to sit down ready to Explore! the story.

EXPLORE!
(20 minutes)

One of the Presenters starts by commenting on the exercises everyone has just done in 'The Restoration Station workout'. Which were the favourite moves? They ask for volunteers to come to the front and demonstrate, and challenge the children to copy the volunteers using the jointed figure they made in 'Workbench welcome'. The Presenters encourage a round of applause for the volunteers, before sending them back to sit down. They invite the children to think of other exercises they could add to the routine, and to demonstrate them using their jointed figure. They congratulate them on their ideas and say they might even add some of those moves to '**The Restoration Station** workout' next time.

The Presenter then asks: 'But what if you weren't able to do any of the exercises? What if you weren't able to move certain parts of your body? How would that make you feel?' They invite responses from the children.

Holding up a Bible, the Presenter explains the children are going to listen to a true story from this very special book, called the Bible. They explain that Christians believe that the Bible tells us true stories about God and how he created the world and people, and that it also tells us about one very special man, called Jesus. (If it's necessary or appropriate to do so, you could say to the children that they may have heard of Jesus, even if they don't know much about him.)

The Presenter, or another member of the team who is a confident reader, reads John 5:1–13 from the Contemporary English Version. (It would be good to read from the Bible that the Presenter shows the children, so that they are reinforcing where the story is coming from.) Make sure the reader has practised it in advance and that they read it slowly and clearly, but also make it sound exciting!

The Presenter explains that, in the city of Jerusalem, there was a pool that was a bit like a spa pool, or a jacuzzi. Can anyone remember its name? (*Beth-za-tha.*) When the bubbles started it would help people who got into the water to feel much better. The Presenter asks why the man in the story hadn't been into the water, and draws out from the responses that he didn't have anyone to help him and it stopped bubbling before he could get there.

The reader reads the story again and, this time, the Presenter invites the children to use their jointed figure as if he were the man in the story.

The Presenter reminds everyone of the Bible verse to remember: **'Anyone who belongs to Jesus has become a new person. The old life is gone; a new life has begun!'** *2 Corinthians 5:17.*

They show it to the children, with some of the words missing, and challenge them to fill in the gaps. They invite everyone to read it together, then ask what it tells us. They say that, like broken objects that are repaired in **The Restoration Station**, Jesus can restore us, too. That's what he did with the man who couldn't walk. No one else could have done that. Only Jesus. Sometimes, people need repairing and restoring on the outside, and sometimes on the inside, too.

Without further comment, the Presenter stands aside to let Chris the carpenter introduce herself or himself and perform the drama 'Meet the no-longer-lame man' (from pages 48 and 49).

When the drama has finished, one of the Presenters introduces and plays the Daisy and Dan animation 'The Potter'. They explain that Daisy is worried about a broken vase. Dan brings someone who can help Daisy to see that things can be repaired, but not in the way we always expect.

EXPLORE DEEPER!
(5–10 minutes)

The Presenters offer the children some questions to help them think more about what they have just seen and heard. They explain the three different ways of exploring the questions and invite the children to choose which exploration area they want to go to: Talking; Creating; Thinking. It is important to make this a free choice – the children can choose whichever approach suits them best.

Today's BIG questions (available to downloaded from **su.org.uk/TheRestorationStation**) are:

- Who did Jesus meet by the bubbling pool?
- What happened next?
- What does this story tell us about Jesus?
- Why did Daisy choose to trust the potter with the broken pieces?

Talking
Talk with the children about the story and the questions. You may need to ask a question to get them started, and steer them back to the questions if they go off track, but encourage the children to do most of the talking. Try not to stifle the children's responses, particularly if their ideas are misguided. Gently and sensitively share your own thoughts and responses with the children, helping them to understand a view that differs from their own. Allow thought and imagination to flow, and ask more questions when a child answers a question. Help them to explore God's Word for themselves!

Creating
Provide the children with artist and making materials, the image from page 51 and the Workshop 2 images (available to download), and encourage them to explore what they have heard, and the questions asked, in a creative way. This is a completely unguided activity – offer whatever help is asked for, but allow the children to create their own response.

Thinking
Have a space set up away from the noise and chatter of the other groups, where children can choose to think quietly and reflect on everything they have seen and heard. Provide copies of the questions, the image from page 51 and also the Workshop 2 images (available to download). You could provide some floor cushions/beanbags or other soft seating, and maybe some soft lighting. Make sure this space is far enough away from the talking so that children who prefer to reflect quietly can do so. Leaders in the thinking area should remind the children that they can talk with their Workbench Leader about what they have been reflecting on during the 'Explore Deeper!' time.

SNACK BREAK
(10 minutes)

Serve the refreshments at the table, with the children sitting down. If you feel brave, you could give each child a paper straw with their drink and challenge them to blow bubbles!

TEAM EXPLORATION
(50 minutes)

The children stay in their Workbench teams for this section. Half the teams should start with 'Go for it!' while the other half start with 'Restoration information'. After about 20 minutes, swap the teams over (allowing up to 10 minutes for the swap to take place). Make sure everyone knows at the beginning that they will get a chance to do everything!

Go for it!
(20 minutes)

Ideally, take the Workbench teams outside, but both of the games could be played indoors if that's not possible. Bearing in mind what is most appropriate for your venue, the number of children you have and what can be achieved in 20 minutes, do one or both of the games outlined. (For either or both games, you may like to give out small prizes linked to the bubble theme in the story, such as mini Aero bars.)

1 Bubble bonanza

This is a relay race, so the children participate in their Workbench teams. As you may have discovered in Workshop 1, some children find it hard to participate in relay races and don't always get it, so be ready to help them and perhaps have a practice run.

Invite each team to line up for the relay race. At the other end of the area and opposite each Workbench team, place a pot of blow bubbles for each child. On the word, 'Go!', invite the first child to run, collect a pot and return to their Workbench team. (They should not open the pots at this stage.) Encourage the next child to do the same, and so on.

You could suggest they get to the bubble pots in different ways and try out different things they can do with different parts of their bodies. For instance, as well as running, they could hop, skip or jump. When they have all collected a pot, encourage the whole team to sit down to indicate they have finished. The first team to do this are the winners. Invite the children to open their pots and blow bubbles. Challenge the Workbench teams to see who can create the best display of bubbles!

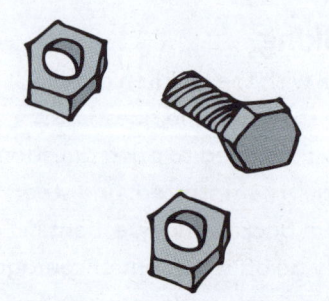

2 Make a choice!

Divide the space you have into three areas. Indicate each area and its boundaries in some way, either with cones, a rope on the ground or tape on the floor, if inside (making sure the tape won't leave a permanent mark on the floor).

Explain to the children (who participate individually) that the three areas marked out represent three places in the story – the bubbling pool, the porch and Jerusalem city. If possible, label each area.

While a leader at the front turns away so they can't see, invite the children to choose one of the three areas and go and stand in it. (If it's practical and safe, and there are not too many children, you could suggest that, if they choose the porch area they could lie down, like the man in the story who was waiting to get into the pool.)

After half a minute or so, when the children have had enough time to choose, the leader at the front should count down from three and, without turning around, say, 'Time to change your mind if you want to!' They wait another 30 seconds, then count down from three again. This time, before turning around, they call out one of the three area names and then turn to face the children. Any children in that area are out.

Keep going for as long as possible – ideally until you have a winner (one child left).